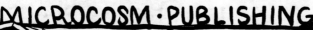

Microcosm Publishing is Portland's most diversified publishing house and distributor with a focus on the colorful, authentic, and empowering. Our books and zines have put your power in your hands since 1996, equipping readers to make positive changes in their lives and in the world around them. Microcosm emphasizes skill-building, showing hidden histories, and fostering creativity through challenging conventional publishing wisdom with books and bookettes about DIY skills, food, bicycling, gender, self-care, and social justice. What was once a distro and record label was started by Joe Biel as an autistic teenager in his bedroom and has become among the oldest independent publishing houses in Portland, OR. We are a politically moderate, centrist publisher in a world that has inched to the right for the past 80 years.

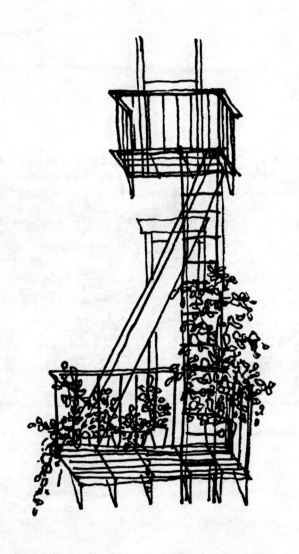

FUGITIVE GARDENS

HOW TO GROW FOOD ON
AN NYC FIRE ESCAPE

Written by
Claire Tuna

Illustrated by
Sheila Lin

Fugitive Gardens

How to Grow Food on an NYC Fire Escape
© Claire Tuna, 2020
This edition © Microcosm Publishing, 2020
ISBN 9781648410215
This is Microcosm # 656
Illustrated by Sheila Lin
Design by Claire Tuna

For a catalog, write or visit:
Microcosm Publishing
2752 N Williams Ave.
Portland, OR 97227
www.Microcosm.Pub

To join the ranks of high-class stores that feature Microcosm titles, talk to your rep: In the U.S. Como (Atlantic), Fujii (Midwest), Book Travelers West (Pacific), Turnaround in Europe, Manda/UTP in Canada, New South in Australia, and GPS in Asia, India, Africa, and South America. Sold to the gift market by Gifts of Nature.

If you bought this on Amazon, we're so sorry because you could have gotten it cheaper and supported a small, independent publisher at Microcosm.Pub
Please add:

Fire escape gardening carries some inherent risks, including (but not limited to) the risk of obstructing an emergency exit or debris falling onto a passerby, both of which could lead to serious injury or death. Moreover, local laws/regulations or the terms of your lease may prohibit maintaining a garden on a fire escape. Accordingly, the author of this publication makes no representations about the safety or legality of any of the practices described herein. The author also encourages all readers to exercise reasonable care to ensure that all of their gardening activities preserve their safety and the safety of others and comply with all applicable laws, regulations, or contractual obligations.

Global labor conditions are bad, and our roots in industrial Cleveland in the 70s and 80s made us appreciate the need to treat workers right. Therefore, our books are MADE IN THE USA.

Introduction

WHEN I SAW THE POST ON CRAIGSLIST—*Free items- moving out!*—I was still moving into a place down the street, holding out for some last kitchen items: a few more tall glasses, a few more cereal bowls. I found that I could get any furnishing I needed second-hand, if I was willing to wait for it.

The poster responded to my email within the hour: *Please text me when downstairs. Stephen*

Upon arrival, Stephen buzzed me in, and I found him a few floors up with his wares sprawled across the stairwell.

"Where are you moving?" I asked.
"California," he said predictably.

He saw me pick up a little terracotta pot, and offered to show me his gardening supplies if I was interested.

He steered me toward a bin holding gardening gloves, a bag of sand, bamboo chop-sticks, and a curious selection of seeds, some in store-bought packets and others in envelopes labeled by hand: scarlet runner beans, radishes, golden berries. As I perused the bin, another woman showed up and started to swiftly stack up the rest of the little pots.

"Wait, have you grown this stuff here? I mean, is it possible?"

He nodded, and shared that he'd grown all sorts of things*, for nine years, until his landlord tore down the installation, which had, admittedly, gotten out of hand. My imagination stirred; I didn't think anything could grow here.

See p.44 for more on Stephen's garden.

8

It turns out Stephen had the right idea, and since our fateful encounter, I have been growing food on the fire escape every summer.

My goal for this guide is to catalog what is possible in this specific environment—a New York City fire escape—and to find out how far people have pushed the concept. I will tell you which plants have succeeded, methods I've learned, and the blueprints and thoughts of a handful of others who, like me, grow food outside their windows, on grates of rusty iron and steel.

9

Supplies

Seeds

Browsing seeds has got to be one of the most exciting parts of gardening. I buy seeds online during the winter from a cooperative in Maine called FedCo, but there are many fascinating seed selections out there. FedCo mails me a paper seed catalog that is full of baroque illustrations of garlic and sensory dispatches like: *This spring in Maine has been cool and rainy, with fires in the woodstove nearly every night and drizzles to downpours what feels like every day since early April...*

I would subscribe to the catalog even if I weren't gardening.

It's hard to believe people like the seed people still exist, but God bless them, they do. Check them out. You will find far more diversity and more regional, heirloom varieties than you could at the hardware store.

My friend (and Master Gardener) Rosemary recommends Hudson Valley Seeds. "Nice people! And I adore their seed packets. They commission an artist for each one."

Of the plants selected in this guide, all are recommended to be grown from seed except for certain herbs (rosemary and mint) and strawberries.

See Planting Calendar on page 12 for the recommended planting dates for our zone.

Soil

Soil is the most costly part of the operation (and the heaviest to take up the stairs). Every year I buy new organic potting soil and seed starting soil for the seeds. Each plant has its own ideal soil requirements and may benefit from additional nutrients or fertilizers, or compost*, none of which are covered in this edition.

*Ethan (p.38) saved food scraps for compost. I admire this move but remain scared of the critters compost might bring into my life.

Containers

All of my plants live in plastic storage tubs and pots found on the sidewalk. Plastic is lightweight, and since these are technically trash to begin with, I don't feel guilty about gouging out drainage holes in the bottom. I recommend strolling through your days with an open mind, waiting for containers to find you. This approach keeps costs down, saves you a trip to the hardware store, and produces less waste than buying new. Once you decide to garden, you can start squirreling away plastic yogurt containers and egg cartons. They are perfect for starting seeds.

Concerns

Fire safety

Repeat after me: No fires! Jokes aside, anyone who gardens on their fire escape is taking on some risk. If you're going to do it, know your escape plan, use common sense, and maintain enough space for yourself and for any others to safely exit the building in case of an emergency.

Getting in trouble

Go ahead and check. Your lease probably does say not to keep plants on the balcony or fire escape. This guide is for those who are opting in anyway. Will you be discovered? Consider your fire escape. Is it visible from the street, or can it only be seen from the backyard? The higher up you live, and the farther from street view, the fewer eyes will notice what you're up to.

Pests? Not really

Fortunately, this does not seem to be a problem in practice. Though I've heard rumors of the occasional squirrel or pigeon causing a ruckus, my only visitors have been doves, bees, and butterflies (cue hairflip).

II

NYC Planting Calendar

Symbols are placed in appropriate weeks for planting*

O start seeds indoors   ● start seeds outside   ⚘ transplant seedlings

	February				March				April				M
Tomato	O	O	O	O						⚘	⚘		
Salad Greens					●	●	●	●	●	●	●	●	●
Basil													
Snap Peas								●	●	●	●	●	●
Strawberry							⚘	⚘	⚘	⚘			
Cucumbers (early)											O	O	
Cucumbers													●
Beans													
Peppers		O	O	O							⚘	⚘	

*Truth be told, there is no magical date for planting things (unless you're using the lunar calendar). Seeds don't care that it's April 22nd. Throughout this guide, planting dates are approximated using this method: The ideal soil or outside temperatures for each planting is pulled from the Cornell vegetable gardening guides (See p.48 for reference). I take that temperature and check it against the average temperatures on Greencast in my zip code, or if the guide refers to the outside temperature, the average daily temperatures on Weatherspark for Brooklyn. The dates below give you a ballpark, but each year is different.

June	July	August	September	October

TRIED & TRUE

In this section, you will find only plants that have definitively succeeded on a sunny fire escape or balcony in New York. Either mine, or one of the other local gardeners featured in the *Blueprints*: Julia, Chris, Ethan, Stephen, and Laura. I've included the most information on tomatoes, which all six of us grow and love. The list is by no means exhaustive, and you are encouraged to experiment with anything that grows in either our hardiness zone (7b) or an adjacent zone if you're what my auntie calls a "zone pusher."

Tomatoes

When to Plant

Start seeds inside 6-8 weeks before transplanting. *Estimated February 15 - March 8.*

Transplant seedlings to the fire escape 1-2 weeks after last frost. *Estimated April 12-19.*

If you miss the boat on growing from seed, pick up a seedling. You'll see tomato starters at plant stores and hardware stores at the beginning of summer.

Picking a Variety

Select a variety that is indeterminate for a constant supply of fruit until the first frost. Fruits of a determinant variety, on the other hand, will ripen all at once. As far as size, I've mostly seen people growing cherry tomatoes.

Container

My tomato lives in a clear, 15-gallon plastic bin I found. Last year I had two tomatoes in that container, but it was pretty crowded. Indeterminate tomatoes grow infinitely large, so one should really be enough for any fire escape.

Tomatoes are buck wild. If I had to pick just one plant to grow every year, it would be the tomato, hands down.

Secrets

Basil can grow merrily around the base of your tomato plant and benefits from the large container size.

Pruning

Use a large container.
See Container

Cage your tomatoes. Cage them with the tallest cage you can find. If you don't cage them, there is no limit to how far and wide they will sprawl. Also, the cage offers protection in the case of storms and wind.

Prune an indeterminate tomato to make it grow tall up a vine instead of short and bushy.
See Pruning

Tomatoes are thirsty. Buy or make a reservoir so your tomato can drink as it pleases.
See Self Watering

Fertilize them puppies. I use Tomato-tone.

Why prune indeterminates?

Indeterminate tomatoes want to grow infinitely every which way. Pruning is the answer. Prune the plant to make it grow tall and in its cage, along a main stem called a "leader," rather than a big hot bushy mess. Pruning your tomato to grow up 1-4 main leaders makes it more portable if you need to move it, as well as space-efficient.

17

You can prune the suckers

But first, let's review the structure of the tomato and how it grows. It's a bit technical, but once you understand it, you will see tomatoes (and pruning) with new eyes.

When your tomato pops up from the dirt, there is one stem in the middle. We call that stem a leader. You will only ever see three types of nodes coming off a leader: leaf nodes, flower nodes (these become the fruit), and suckers. Suckers grow diagonally, bisecting the angle between a leaf node and the main stem. (See right)

Suckers start off as these cute little things that are easy to pinch off with your finger. Each one, if left to grow, becomes a new leader, growing its own leaf nodes, flower nodes, and...suckers! This is what I mean when I say the tomato grows infinitely. It's a fractal.

Some people eliminate every sucker and grow tomatoes up a single leader. Adequately supported tomatoes, pruned to a single leader, will likely grow taller than you. In the fire escape context, you may only have one tomato, so it's a good idea to aim for 2-4 leaders in case one of them suffers from disease or snaps in two in a tropical storm.

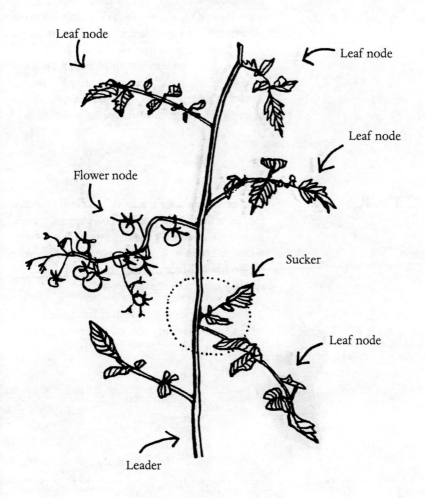

Leaf node

Leaf node

Leaf node

Flower node

Sucker

Leaf node

Leader

19

Self Watering

On a hot summer day, my tomato drains 1.5 gallons of water from the reservoir. The self-watering system allows me to skip a day or two of watering when I need to and to bank rainwater.

The design here is haphazard, adaptable, and based entirely on the supplies I had/found, but I do hope the principles are of use. If you are implementing a version of this design, do so before you transplant your tomato.

The Rig

The inner container is a 15-gallon plastic storage bin. In its floor, I have carved holes approximately 3-inches diameter for the roots to escape into the water reservoir (the outer container). To prevent too much soil from falling through the holes, I slapped some packing tape over them.

The outer container is a similar plastic storage bin with a small drainage hole carved about 8 inches from the bottom.

Watering

Some handy folks use a tube to pipe water down to the reservoir, but I just jam a wooden kitchen spoon* between the two containers, wedge it sideways, and pour water through the gap it creates. Once the reservoir is full, the roots will make their way down there to suck up the water. Until that time, water the tomato from the top.

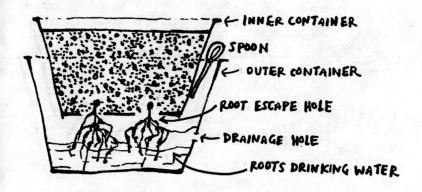

INNER CONTAINER
SPOON
OUTER CONTAINER
ROOT ESCAPE HOLE
DRAINAGE HOLE
ROOTS DRINKING WATER

*I can't say that I particularly recommend the spoon route, but it demonstrates that you don't need to buy any fancy equipment to set up a self-watering container.

Herbs

Basil

Harvest from the top and pinch off flowers if you like it bushy.

Basil is perfectly happy on my fire escape, and I see big bushy manes of it in the planterboxes of nearly every outdoor dining pop-up in the neighborhood. Plant basil around the base of your tomato plant; those two are compatible, and the basil grows bigger in a large container. Alternatively, you can grow basil in a container as shallow as 8 inches deep. I grew both Thai Basil and Genovese Basil this year, and the Thai Basil took over and shaded out the Genovese. Next time I'm sticking with only the Genovese, which I favor in the kitchen.

Start seeds indoor 4-8 weeks before last frost.
Feb 8 - March 8.

Sow seeds directly when night temperatures are above 55 degrees. After May 15.

Cilantro I never have seen on display in the neighborhood. My cilantro grows precisely four leaves before it tips over sideways and croaks.

Mint

Mint is low maintenance and grows like a weed. Keep it in its own container so that it doesn't choke out its roommates.

Grow from a starter plant or cutting any old time.

Parsley

Rumor has it that Chris (p.36) grew parsley from a nursery plant on his fire escape without any issues.

Direct sow as early as 2-3 weeks before last frost (March 15-March 22)

Rosemary

Rosemary is another hearty* option that I see doing well in containers all around town, and it's a perennial, so you can bring it inside during the winter and keep it for the following year. It is said to be difficult to start from seed, so picking up a starter plant or propagating a cutting is recommended.

Grow from a starter plant or cutting any time.

*My mom once replanted a rosemary bush after leaving it uprooted in a garbage pile for two years. It grew.

Salad Greens

When to Plant

As soon as you can work the soil—i.e. whenever the soil is no longer frozen or soggy—plant seeds directly in the garden. For a continual harvest, sow seeds every couple of weeks until around mid-October, or one month before last frost.

The seed packet will tell you how to space the seeds, but if you're in a fun mood, you can just sprinkle and scatter them about however you like, and then cover with a bit of soil (1/4 inch). It is not a precise art, and I've found it's okay to crowd them. If you end up thinning them out later, it's all ultimately edible.

Picking a Variety

This year I planted Perpetual Spinach Chard and Roquette Arugula. More varieties (e.g. mustard greens, escarole, radicchio, dandelion greens, frisée, mizuna, mâche) could make for a more interesting salad. Check around for heat resistant varieties for peak summer harvests.

Harvest

When the leaves are mature (3+ inches tall), you can cut off the outer leaves and leave the baby leaves to grow from the center of the plant. You can keep doing this over and over again, or harvest the whole plant and reseed all season.

Container

Compared to tomatoes, salad greens grow relatively shallow roots. To save on soil requirements, you can use a shallow container with a large surface area (as shallow as 8 inches) for most salad greens.

25

Peas

When to Plant

You can sow seeds in spring as soon as you can work the soil, though germination is optimal with warmer temperatures, so it's okay to take your time.

Sow directly March 20 - May 15

Picking a Variety

Bush varieties grow smaller than **vining varieties** and do not require trellising, making them the easier choice for a container garden.

Container

You can use a container on the shallow side with peas, like a window box container. Select something at least 6 inches deep, and leave 2-6 inches between each plant.

Cucumbers

When to Plant

Cucumbers, much like my friend Abby, are sensitive to the cold, so wait to sow seeds outside until soil reaches 65 degrees. *After May 15th.*

If you're extra eager, start seeds inside 3-4 weeks before transplanting.
April 17-April 24.

Picking a Variety

As with peas, **bush varieties** grow more compactly than vining varieties, so they do not require trellising, making them the easier choice for a container garden. **Vining varieties** require a trellis or cage for support.

Container

Grow 1 cucumber per 3-5 gallon pot.

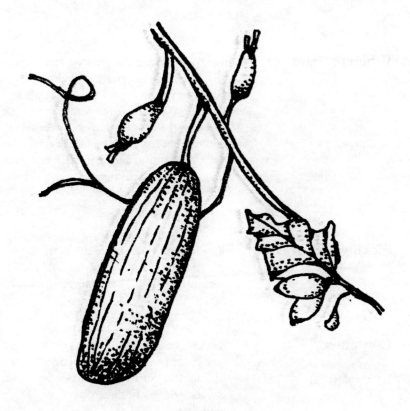

Strawberries

When to Plant

For transient renters, growing strawberries from seed is not recommended. Buy a strawberry plant from a nursery at winter's end for summer fruit. Strawberries live through the winter, and this year's fruit comes from last year's buds. You can buy a plant online or at a local nursery and plant once the ground has thawed.
Transplant after March 15th.

Picking a Variety

June-bearing varieties are the most popular choice in New York. They ripen all at once, around June time, as the name suggests.

Container

Strawberries do not require deep containers, so opt for containers with a larger surface area instead. Six or more inches depth will do, and you can fit three plants per 10-inch container.

Remove runners cascading from your plant strawberry plant to maximize yields the first year.

Honorable Mentions

Peppers

Advice from Chris: Plant your peppers at least six inches apart, use stakes to keep them straight, and fertilize.

Mixed reviews, y'all. I grew sweet peppers, and sadly, they did not taste nearly as good as the ones from the store. On the other hand, Chris (p. 36) grew both sweet and hot peppers this year with great joy. If you're a spicy pepper person (you know who you are), you might want to give peppers a whirl on the fire escape, but the general public can skip.

Start seeds indoors 8-10 weeks before transplanting them. February 8- March 1

Transplant 2-3 weeks after last frost, when the weather has stabilized.
April 19 - April 26

Pole beans

Beans can certainly grow on a fire escape, but I suspect they would taste better if they were tomatoes.

The act of burying a straight-up bean and watching it grow into a beanstalk was one of the highlights of 2020 in my book, but I had moderate yields growing *Seychelles pole beans* on the fire escape. I must admit that I love the way they dangle.

Plant when the soil temperature has warmed above 60 degrees. After May 14

BLUEPRINTS

When the sun came out in May, I planted salad greens and a tomato starter. As I watched them grow, I noticed my neighbors, stripped almost entirely of access to public space, were pressing into every inch of private space they had. Shoebox yards and balconies that were usually empty displayed people I had never seen before laying on blankets, sitting back in chairs, sunbathing or making phone calls. From above, it looked like a scene out of *Where's Waldo*.

In July, I began to scout out other fire escapes for this collection, scanning roadside apartments for flashes of green wherever I went. I left notes outside of promising buildings and send emails to gardeners I found on the internet.

The blueprints that follow are based on drawings generously provided by five gardeners across Brooklyn, in Crown Heights, Bed Stuy, Greenpoint, and Boerum Hill. Perhaps due to the transient nature of city dwellers, the gardens are mostly limited to spring and summer plantings. Some are more over-the-top, whereas others are simple. They are here to give you a hint of what is feasible, but what you grow, and how you grow it, is entirely up to you.

Chris

"Excuse me, do you live here?" I ask the tall fellow who is warily watching me from the sidewalk.

"No," he says.

Disappointed, I rest my bike against the wrought iron fence and take some pictures of the quaint display anyway. A light, silver wind chime is hanging from the stairs above, and healthy cherry tomatoes are climbing up tall, well-pruned leaders. Fluffy flowers spill over the edge of the window boxes. Not to mention, the window is cracked open a few inches. Meaning, somebody is home? I tell him I'd like to deliver a note to the gardener.

"Ok. It's my garden. What do you want."

These warm words kick off my conversation with Chris. Five minutes later, we are swiping through photos of his creation: thriving basil (and pesto), a butterfly visiting the thyme, and large peppers growing up against the red brick wall. Ten minutes later, he is getting to work spreading epoxy in a crack in his fender (the reason he came outside in the first place) and telling me I can let myself into the apartment if I want to take a look.

"Just don't like, steal my stuff."

The place is tidy, and a raggedy cat named Stanley, whose left eye closes more than his right, follows me closely around as I walk toward the fire escape. I holler to Chris that I am petting the cat so he won't think I'm casing the place.

"He's a nice cat, isn't he? Give him some catnip."

36

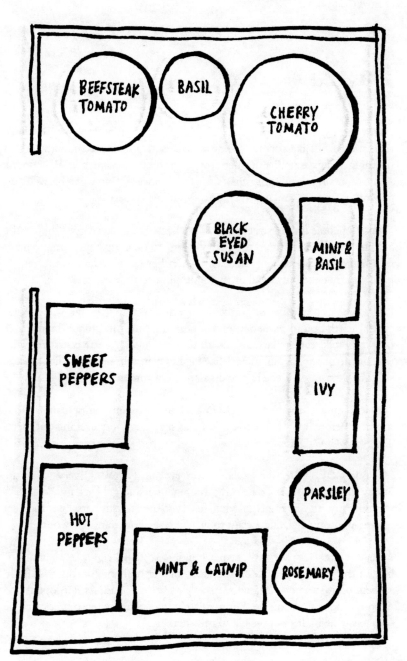

BEEFSTEAK TOMATO

BASIL

CHERRY TOMATO

BLACK EYED SUSAN

MINT & BASIL

SWEET PEPPERS

IVY

PARSLEY

HOT PEPPERS

MINT & CATNIP

ROSEMARY

Laura

Laura and I meet in a park on a July day so hot that any form of outdoor recreation feels like torture (I know because I got dressed for a run that morning and gave up the moment my shoes hit the pavement). We sit in the shade on neon yellow camp chairs with an awkwardly large gap between us, peel off our masks, and get to talking about her garden.

"I talk to people on the street all the time because I'm always out there," she admits. People, sometimes drunk, are prone to greeting her or trapping her in a lengthy conversation, especially when her cat Horchata is present. "I have nightmares in my head of them jumping on the railing..."

Laura reports a number of curiosities, some which may be familiar to your typical earth-bound gardener, and others that are the unique inheritance of us sky folk; caterpillars, aphids, dead birds, and cigarette butts from her upstairs neighbor have all materialized in her plants. In spite of it all, she says, she'd be devastated if she had to dismantle the garden.

"I'm in a studio," she begins, "I'm in a studio, with another person, for four months. Before it got really hot out, I was spending every evening out there. That's my COVID life."

Her non-COVID life, she explains, was far more active. "Every weekend, Friday through Sunday, I'd be out climbing. I need to get back out," she says wistfully, noting that the Gunks had just reopened to climbers. "But the heat has me unmotivated, and I want to wait and see how things play out."

After the interview, we walk to her building so that I can take a picture of her on the fire escape. It's on the front of her building, on the first floor, suspended just a few feet above the garbage-can lids. As she opens the window and crawls outside, I immediately understand why so many people stop to say hello. It's impossible to miss her.

38

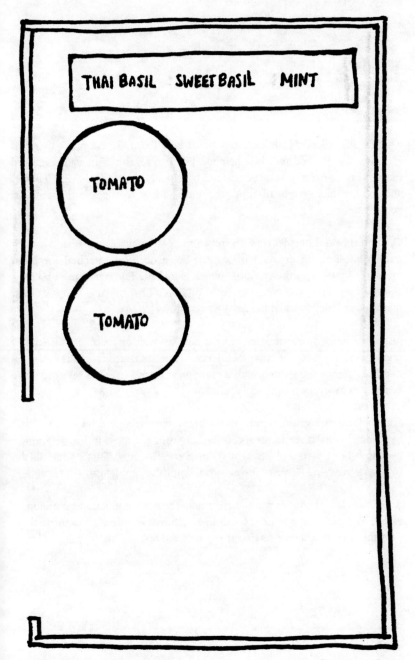

THAI BASIL   SWEET BASIL   MINT

TOMATO

TOMATO

Ethan

There's this balcony I always see when I bike from Greenpoint to Crown Heights. Yes, it's technically a balcony, but I think the dimensions are fire escapey enough. On several occasions I have puzzled at the tall, vining plants and the fort-like system of rope strung up ad hoc to support them. What could it be?

One afternoon, I decide to reach out to the gardener. I leave a handwritten note requesting an email, with a little sprig of mint attached for good measure. I tape it to the mailbox, which is locked. The next time I bike by, about a week later, the note is gone, and I haven't heard back. I hope at least that the gardener found it before the mint shriveled up.

Just at the exact moment when I forget that I'm waiting for an email, Ethan's message comes, and our correspondence begins. I can tell from his messages that he watches the garden with a close and curious eye. He says the same bee comes by every morning.

Some plants we grow. Some plants grow themselves. Ethan writes that he noticed squash seedlings sprouting up from compost in his girlfriend's grandmother's yard and brought them home to grow. That's what all the rope was for, tying "little twine hammocks for the rapidly growing fruit."

A few days later he sends me a correction—the squash is actually a melon. A melon that looks, to me, like cantaloupe. Ultimately, Ethan gives the melons a thumbs down and reports that they never did taste right.

40

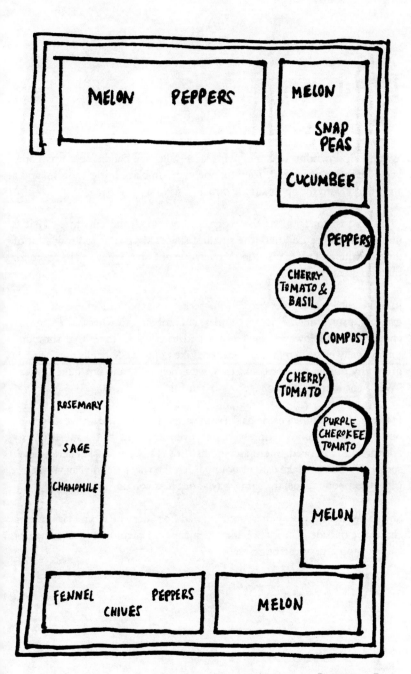

Julia

When I sit down for a glass of wine with Julia, she hands me a wax paper bag containing one cherry tomato, one purplish-black blade of shiso, and a strawberry with the approximate dimensions of a pinto bean.

"The goal is not to grow the biggest something," she tells me. "That is not possible, because I have the smallest space. My goal is to grow a lot of different things. I plant way too many in one pot, so there won't be room for them to grow big."

In terms of designing her garden, she picks seeds that catch her fancy from catalogs, usually including her staples: cucumbers, strawberries, tomatoes, and snap peas. However, she's not afraid to try something that shouldn't theoretically be grown on a fire escape. Like potatoes. She tells me she once grew tiny purple potatoes, and they were delicious, and not quite a meal. "Well," she laughs, "the foliage was beautiful."

I tell her about a time I came back from vacation to find the tomatoes grown out of control, almost entirely tipped over, and how the plant-sitter, my friend, hadn't noticed. She understands. "It's really personal. There's never somebody that can take care of your garden the way that you can. You can't expect someone to feel the same way about it as you do."

She shares her harvest with a rabbit named Bob, a rescue from Harlem who "hates the outside." Lucky Bob likes to snack on a cucumber slice, or half of a cherry tomato, or carrot greens.

42

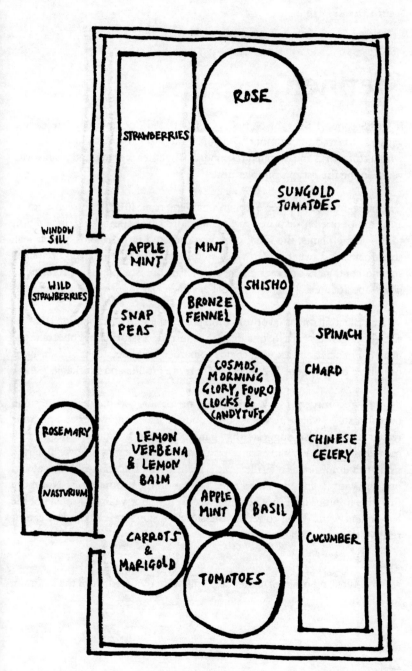

Stephen

It was Stephen I thought of first when I started documenting fire escape gardens. I texted the number from the Craigslist post (p.8), hoping that it would still work, and Stephen responded. Together we revisited his favorite years on the fire escape. Simpler times.

On the right, you can see Stephen's garden from 2014*. I've seen photos, and I'm not one bit surprised that his landlord came a-knocking. In addition to the edible plants, the fire escape was carpeted in marigolds, purple-leaf shamrocks, and sweet potato vines so full and lush that one can no longer see the containers or grating beneath. Turns out Stephen is a professional landscape architect. I asked him what advice he has for fire escape gardeners.

When reflecting on his favorite plantings over the years, he mentions that his sixth-floor garden got a lot of sun, so the most successful plants could take the heat. He had better luck with cherry tomatoes over beefsteaks and shishitos over large bell peppers, "because they're more prolific and snackable."

Stephen recommends that gardeners opt for large containers over small ones, because "when the soil is contiguous, it shares the water and microbe resources." He also suggests that gardeners keep a saucer beneath each container to avoid spilling water on unsuspecting victims below. "I started using fish emulsion as a fertilizer. It is really great, but stinky. I had watered one day with it, and the excess rained down on the ground floor. Not more than five minutes later, my neighbor was at my door yelling at me! I got the bleach and went down to rectify the situation. Lesson learned. Use saucer reservoirs and no fish emulsion!"

*Many bulbs and other ornamental plants were removed from the diagram, for simplicity.

44

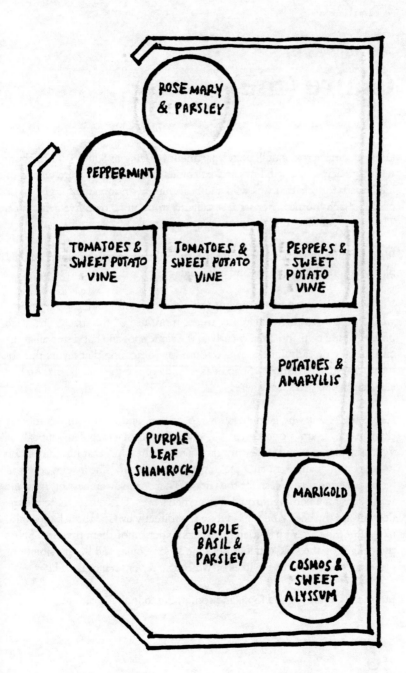

Claire (me)

Once, I came across a dull, boxy apartment building in South Williamsburg with bars across the windows and balconies. The balconies were devoid of life, except for one that was wild and brimming with tomatoes. Eight, to be precise. Each loomed over six feet tall and stood in its own five-gallon pot. They were full-size tomatoes, too.

It's a tempting prospect, devoting the summer to tomatoes alone. I could plant eight funky heirlooms and call it a day.

I grew a little more than tomatoes this season, and looking back on it, I would do a few things differently to get more use of the space. The salad greens would be planted really early in the same spot and harvested all at the end of May or early June to make room for something that favors the hot weather (e.g. a cucumber). Snap peas would replace the pole beans. And I'd slip a strawberry in somewhere.

It's no big secret why gardeners love to garden, and even with my modest sky-garden, I am no different. There's the Tamagotchi-like appeal of watching plants evolve under my care. There's the smell that fills the air and lingers on my hand even after picking just one tomato. The instant access to herbs and greens too fresh for the fridge. There's the awareness of light, the way I sense fall coming through the garden's eyes. Of course, there are the flowers and the bees. And the ladybug sent directly by God to suck up aphids like a Roomba after I had tried for weeks to get rid of them myself. There's the delight of the seed catalogs (and the seed people) and the possibility of growing fruits or herbs the likes of which I've never seen or tasted.

But mostly, there is good food, and something to look forward to.

46

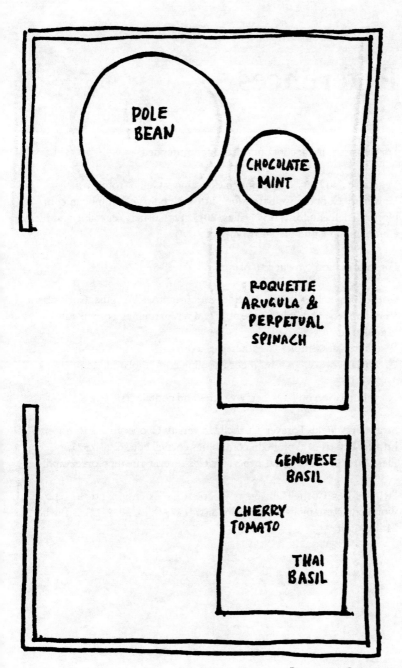

POLE BEAN

CHOCOLATE MINT

ROQUETTE ARUGULA & PERPETUAL SPINACH

GENOVESE BASIL

CHERRY TOMATO

THAI BASIL

BLUEPRINTS • CLAIRE (ME)

References

For information on container sizes recommended:

Vegetable and Herb Gardening in Containers Guide from Cornell University Cooperative Extension . https://cpb-us-e1.wpmucdn.com/blogs.cornell.edu/dist/f/575/files/2015/12/Cornell-Vegetable-and-Herb-Gardening-in-Containers-25g3vpj.pdf

For information on when to plant:

Cornell Vegetable Growing Guides for: Tomatoes, Arugula, Cucumbers, Peas, Peppers, and Pole beans. http://www.gardening.cornell.edu/homegardening
Weather Spark. https://weatherspark.com/
GreenCast. https://www.greencastonline.com/tools/soil-temperature

For information on strawberry varities and containers:

Strawberry Yields Forever. Cornell University Cooperative Extension. https://cpb-us-e1.wpmucdn.com/blogs.cornell.edu/dist/f/575/files/2016/07/newlogostrawberry-yields-forever-1ue4bpp-or9czw.pdf

Strawberries. Cornell University Cooperative Extension. https://cpb-us-e1.wpmucdn.com/blogs.cornell.edu/dist/f/575/files/2015/12/5strawberries-21dju94.pdf

Acknowledgements

Julia, Ethan, Laura, Stephen, Chris: Thank you for sharing your gardens and time. Thank you, Sheila. Your illustrations brought oodles of personality to these pages. Thank you to Joe and the team at Microcosm. I feel lucky to have found you. Matthew, thank you for your artistic eye. Your notes hurt so good. Hannah, thank you for getting down and dirty with the language and formatting of this zine. Thank you Rosemary for lending your gardening expertise. And Aimée, for your feedback and perpetual hype. Thank you to the gardeners in my family who showed me the way, and all the growers who have come before. Thank you to the memoir workshop peeps for keeping the energy flowing during quarantine: Alex, Annie Lyall, Frank, Hannah, Lara, Sharon, Siddhi, and Siobahn. Thank you, RGH. You know what you did. Andrew and Eric, thanks for sending selfies with the plants when we go out of town. You are fun tomato uncles. And John, thank you for your steady care, and for pushing this guide to be better.

Finally, thank you to my landlord for not evicting me (yet).